Nov 16

For my family, with love —R.E.H.

To my mother, illustrator Sharon Lerner —M.P.

Millbrook Press
A division of Lerner Publishing Group, Inc.
241 First Avenue North
Minneapolis, MN 55401 USA

For reading levels and more information, look up this title at www.lernerbooks.com.

Design by Zachary Marell and Kimberly Morales
Main body text set in HandySans 22/27.
The illustrations in this book were created using cut paper collage with watercolor.

Library of Congress Cataloging-in-Publication Data

Names: Hirsch, Rebecca E., author. | Posada, Mia, illustrator.
Title: Plants can't sit still / by Rebecca E. Hirsch ; illustrated by Mia Posada.
Other titles: Plants can not sit still
Description: Minneapolis : Millbrook Press, [2016]
Identifiers: LCCN 2015036957 | ISBN 9781467780315 (lb : alk. paper) | ISBN 9781512411096 (eb pdf)
Subjects: LCSH: Plants—Juvenile literature. | Growth (Plants)—Juvenile literature.
Classification: LCC QK49 .H5384 2016 | DDC 580—dc23

LC record available at http://lccn.loc.gov/2015036957

Manufactured in the United States of America
1-37643-18739-3/1/2016

Plants Can't Sit Still

REBECCA E. HIRSCH

ILLUSTRATIONS BY

MIA POSADA

M Millbrook Press/Minneapolis

Plants don't have feet
or fins or wings,

yet they can **move**
in many ways.

Look closely and you'll discover that **plants**

can't sit still.

Plants can wiggle.

As seedlings start to grow,

they squirm out of spring soil,

unfold their leaves,

and **reach**
for the warmth
and the light.

Plants can **creep**.

They **slither** underground

or **crawl** through tall grass

searching for the things
that all plants need:
water, sunshine, and
room to grow.

And as they **search,** plants can **climb** a fence

or **walk up** a wall.

Plants can **hide**
from a hungry
grasshopper

or surprise a fly.
Snap!

Some plants **sleep** at night,

leaves **nodding,**

flowers folding.

Others **wake** with the stars
and **lift** their faces to the moon.

Plants can **tumble** on a *breeze*.

Whoosh!

As they bounce along,

seeds sprinkle out.

Plants even **explode!**
They **fling** their seeds into the world
to make new plants.

A seed is a plant
built for travel.

Seeds can **whirl**
like helicopters

or **float** on
parachutes

or **glide** on papery wings.

But they **can't sit still.**

Seeds **hitchhike**
on your sock

or on a fox's bushy tail.

They take a **ride**
inside a bear.

Seeds set sail. *Sploosh!*

Down the river, past *swaying* trees, into the wide ocean.

Drifting. Waiting . . .
for what all plants need:
water, sunshine, and room
to grow.

When the seed finds a spot,
the seedling **squirms** out.

It **unfolds** its leaves.

It **reaches** for the warmth and the light.

And it keeps on **moving**—because

plants
can't sit
still.

MORE ABOUT PLANTS

Plants share our world, but you might be surprised at all they can do. You may never have noticed that plants can move. The reason is simple: their movement is usually very slow compared to yours.

Plants move to get the things they need to survive, like a spot in the sunshine with plenty of water. Sunlight powers the growing plant. Leaves catch sunlight and turn it into food and energy, a process called photosynthesis. Water is important because it makes up most of a plant's tissues. Plants suck up water through their roots and send the water to their stems, leaves, and flowers.

Movement also helps plants reproduce. Some plants open their flowers at a certain time of day or night to attract bees, moths, or other pollinators. These helper animals spread pollen from one flower to another, which allows new seeds to form. The seeds must then move away from their parent plant to find their own, uncrowded place in the world.

Although scientists understand the reasons for many plant movements, sleep movements are mysterious. It is not always clear why plants fold or droop at night. For some plants, this may help keep them warm during the dark, cold night. For others, sleep movements may prevent nighttime animals from munching on them.

Want to see evidence of plant movement for yourself? Just go outside and look around. Ask yourself: Are any of the plants climbing to reach the sunlight? Do any fold their leaves at night? Look carefully at any seeds you find. How are those seeds built to travel? Look closely and you will discover for yourself the many ways plants use movement to survive and grow.

Here is more information about the plants in this book, listed in the order in which the plants appear.

Sunflower (*Helianthus annus*) produces big seeds that are fun to grow. When a sunflower seed starts to grow, or germinates, the plant must orient itself. The root senses the tug of gravity and grows down. The stem senses both gravity and light. It grows up, away from the gravity and toward the light. The plant must grow toward the light so the leaves can carry out photosynthesis.

Common milkweed (*Asclepias syriaca*) and the **garden strawberry (*Fragaria x ananassa*)** take over new ground by forming colonies. The plants in the colony appear to be separate, but they are all connected. Some, like milkweed, are connected by underground runners. Others, like the garden strawberry, are connected by aboveground runners.

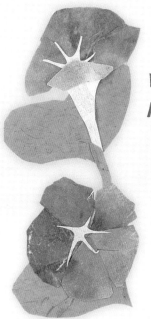

Morning glory (*Ipomoa purpurea*) and **English ivy (*Hedera helix*)** are lazy. They climb over other plants to reach sunlight rather than supporting themselves. Like all climbing plants, they have an excellent sense of touch. When a morning glory tendril brushes against something, the tendril coils up and squeezes. When an English ivy stem comes in contact with a surface, it grows roots at that spot. The roots ooze a gooey cement to attach themselves to the surface. Other climbing plants come equipped with hooks, sticky pads, or touch-sensitive leaves that grab like hands.

Sensitive plant (*Mimosa pudica*) is sometimes called "touch-me-not" and for good reason. With the touch of a finger, a gentle shake, or the nibble of an insect, it folds its leaves against its stem, like tiny, green dominoes. The action of one plant folding can trigger a neighboring sensitive plant to fold its leaves. The signal travels from plant to plant until the leaves of all the nearby sensitive plants are tucked away. The leaves will unfold again in about twenty minutes.

Venus flytrap (*Dionaea muscipula*) grows in swamps where the soil is poor. Catching insects provides nutrients that the plant needs. When an insect lands in the right spot, the leaf snaps shut in less than a second. After that, the plant takes its time. A week might pass while Venus Flytrap digests its catch. Only after the meal is over will the leaf open again.

Common bean (*Phaseolus vulgaris*) and **tulip (*Tulipa* genus)** both move with the twenty-four-hour cycle of day and night. Bean leaves droop at night and tulip flowers close. The word for this type of movement is *circadian*, which in Latin means "about a day." The plants know day from night by sensing changes in light and temperature. Oddly, the movements will continue even if the plant is kept in a special chamber where light and temperature don't change.

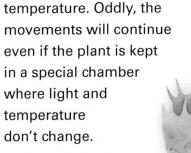

Moonflower (*Ipomoea genus*) opens at night so that it can be pollinated by night-flying moths. The bloom lasts for just one night. When the morning sun touches the petals, the flower closes and dies. Seeds grow inside the withered flowers. The moonflower is a close relative of the morning glory, which opens in the morning and is pollinated by bees and other day-flying insects.

Russian thistle (*Salsola tragus*) grows in dry land where there are few trees and shrubs to get in its way. When it is ready to spread its seeds, the plant breaks off at the base and curls into a crispy ball. It is then called a tumbleweed. It rolls over hills and valleys, pushed by wind. Inside are thirty thousand to fifty thousand seeds that are scattered as the twiggy tumbleweed rolls.

Squirting cucumber (*Ecballium elaterium*) fruits—the part of the plant that holds the seeds—look like hairy cucumbers. These cucumbers can shoot seeds the length of a school bus. As the cucumber ripens, it fills with a slimy juice. The pressure inside the fruit grows and grows until the cucumber explodes off the plant, squirting a slimy, seedy trail behind it.

Red maple (*Acer rubrum*) seeds are packaged inside double propellers. Each propeller has a swollen end filled with a seed and a papery end. The two halves split apart. When the wind shakes the tree, the propeller spins. The seeds can land in all kinds of places, which is why you might find a maple tree growing on a roof or in a crack in the sidewalk.

Dandelion (*Taraxacum officinale*) seeds are carried on the wind by the thousands, each seed attached to its own parachute. Dandelion flowers form a puffy white ball. The flowers will open on dry days, when the wind might carry the seeds for miles. In rainy weather, the flowers close because the parachutes don't work on wet days.

Asian climbing gourd (Alsomitra macrocarpa) is a vine that climbs high in the rain forest. From the vines hang football-sized gourds, each packed with hundreds of seeds. Paper-thin wings allow the seed to glide in wide circles through the forest. The seed may have inspired the design of early aircraft and gliders.

Beggar-ticks (Bidens pilosa) and **stick-tight (Desmodium cuspidatum)** travel with animals and people. Take a walk through a meadow, and you may find these hitchhikers clinging to your socks or sweater. You probably didn't notice that you were giving them a ride. And you'll probably pick them off and drop them on the ground. You've just helped a plant spread its seeds.

Cocklebur (Xanthium strumarium) or a similar hitchhiker may have inspired the invention of Velcro. In 1948, a Swiss engineer went hiking with his dog. They both came home covered with burs. He studied the burs and noticed they attached themselves to clothes and fur by little hooks. That inspired him to invent a new kind of fastener.

Raspberries (Rubus genus) package their seeds inside a tasty fruit. The fruit gets eaten, and so the seeds travel inside an animal. Hard coats allow the seeds to survive the ride through the bear's stomach and intestine. The seeds come out unharmed in the animal's poop.

Coconut palm (Cocos nucifera) makes a fruit that contains everything needed for a long trip at sea. The hard shell keeps out salt water. Inside the coconut is a supply of food and water and a pocket of air to help it stay afloat.

Author's Note

To write this book, I needed to learn how and why plants move and also watch them in action. I read widely on plant movement, including an old book on climbing plants by naturalist Charles Darwin. One of my favorite sources was a series of articles on noteworthy plants by botanist Wayne P. Armstrong (http://waynesword.palomar.edu/worthypl.htm), which pointed me to particular plants with interesting abilities. As much as possible, I observed plants directly—in my garden and in meadows and woods near my house. If I couldn't watch a plant directly, I sought out videos showing its movements. One website that was particularly helpful was the Plants-in-Motion website of plant biologist Roger Hangarter, which has time-lapse videos of a wide range of plants.

Glossary

cement: a substance that glues things together

colonies: a group of similar plants living or growing together

germinates: begins to grow from a seed

gliders: aircrafts without engines that glide on air currents

gravity: the force of attraction between Earth and objects on its surface

hitchhike: to travel by securing a free ride from a passing traveler

orient: to adjust the direction of growth. Plants use gravity and sunlight to sense which direction to grow.

parachute: a folding device made of lightweight material that helps objects travel on the wind. The parachute of a dandelion seed is made of silky hairs.

pollen: tiny, dustlike particles formed inside of flowers

pollinated: transferred pollen within a flower or to another flower. Pollination helps flowers make seeds.

propellers: devices with rotating blades, such as the blades of a helicopter

reproduce: to produce offspring. Plants reproduce by making seeds.

runners: slender creeping stems

seedling: a young plant

tendril: a curly, winding stem that helps some plants climb

withered: shriveled and faded

More Information

Books

Aston, Dianna Hutts. *A Seed Is Sleepy*. San Francisco: Chronicle Books, 2014.
Learn fascinating facts about seeds and how they grow into plants.

Jenson-Elliott, Cindy. *Weeds Find a Way*. New York: Beach Lane Books, 2014.
Explore the many ways that weeds adapt to their environment and send their seeds into the world.

Macken, JoAnn Early. *Flip, Float, Fly: Seeds on the Move*. New York: Holiday House, 2008.
Learn more about the ways seeds have of traveling to new places.

Salas, Laura Purdie. *A Leaf Can Be . . .* Minneapolis: Millbrook Press, 2012.
Discover the different roles that leaves can play throughout the seasons.

Websites

Plants in Motion
http://plantsinmotion.bio.indiana.edu/plantmotion/starthere.html
Watch time-lapse videos showing plants wiggling, twirling, sleeping, and more.

Shooting Seeds, Burrowing Seeds
http://www.pbs.org/wnet/nature/the-seedy-side-of-plants-video-shooting-seeds-burrowing-seeds/4665/
Check out a video showing how squirting cucumber and other exploding plants spread their seeds.

Venus Flytrap Catches Flies
http://www.discovery.com/tv-shows/life/videos/venus-flytrap-catches-flies/
This video takes you up close as a Venus flytrap catches a fly.